The Last Supper
and Other Bible Favorites

ARCTURUS

Jesus Enters Jerusalem

John 12:12-13 The next day a great crowd who had come to the feast heard that Jesus was coming to Jerusalem. So they took branches of palm trees and went out to meet him.

In preparation for the eight-day Passover festival, the city of Jerusalem was bustling. All kinds of people were flocking there from far and wide, and the narrow streets were alive with the latest story about Jesus. It was said that he had brought a man back to life who had been dead and buried for four days! Then the news spread that Jesus was on his way to Jerusalem. An excited crowd soon set off to meet him.

Meanwhile, Jesus and his disciples had reached a village some way from Jerusalem. Jesus asked two of his disciples to go into the village and bring him a young donkey that was tethered there. "If anyone asks what you are doing," said Jesus, "tell them that the Master needs him and will send him back soon."

"Hey! What are you doing?" shouted a man as the disciples untied the donkey. "The Master wants him," replied the disciples.

"That's fine, then," replied the man. "But be careful with him as no one has ever ridden that donkey before."

The disciples spread their cloaks on the donkey's back to make a saddle for Jesus. As soon as Jesus climbed on to the young donkey's back, it was calm and stepped forward proudly.

Many years before this, the prophet Zechariah had foretold that one day the true king would come to Jerusalem, not galloping on a horse, but riding peacefully on a donkey. People knew this, and everyone who saw Jesus on that day believed that he was the true king.

A large crowd hurried to join Jesus and his disciples as they entered Jerusalem. Some went ahead and some even threw down their cloaks so that the donkey could walk over them. Others cut down palm branches from the trees and spread them on the road as the donkey carried Jesus slowly into the city.

"Hosanna!" shouted the people. "Here comes our long-promised king! God bless the one who comes in the name of the Lord!"

The crowd carried on through the streets to the beautiful temple where Jews from all over the world gathered to praise God.

Jesus in the Temple

Jesus arrived at the courtyard of the temple. He looked around but, as it was evening and Jerusalem was so crowded, he and his disciples went back to Bethany to stay with friends for the night.

The following morning, Jesus and his disciples returned to Jerusalem and Jesus went straight back to the temple. Although the big courtyard was open to all, it should have been a quiet place where people could come to pray and learn about God. Instead, there was a terrible noise. Animals bleated and mooed, birds twittered, market traders shouted, and people crossed the

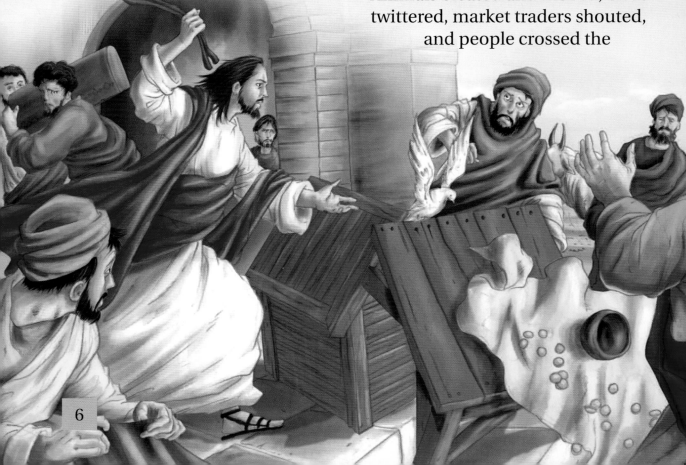

courtyard with their animals, using it as a shortcut.

Jesus could see that the traders were selling animals to pilgrims to use as offerings to God, and charging many times the normal price for them. The money-changers were cheating, too. Every Jew had to pay a "temple tax" at Passover time, but those who changed the pilgrims' coins were making a big profit. Some people believed that the priests themselves were behind much of the trading.

Jesus was very angry. The poor were being cheated, and God's house was being used as a corrupt market. Fearlessly, he strode forward and shooed away the oxen, sheep, and doves, then he began overturning all the tables, scattering coins everywhere. Next, he turned away the people who were using the temple as a shortcut through the streets.

Everyone stopped in their tracks as Jesus exclaimed, "How dare these people trade in the temple?

They should sell their goods elsewhere! Thieves and money-changers have no place in a house of prayer!"

Pilgrims looked on in amazement. Jesus was being incredibly brave, defying some of the most powerful people in the land. The priests and leaders were furious with Jesus. It was their job to keep order in the temple, not his, but they were wary of him because so many people followed him and believed that he was the Son of God.

The traders had a reason to be cross with Jesus because, under the Law of Moses, people were required to offer animal sacrifices. Those traveling a long way to the temple in Jerusalem would take money with them to buy an animal for their offering. So it was not wrong for men to sell the animals, but people knew that Jesus was right that they should have been selling them outside the temple area.

Did you know?

A pilgrim is a person who goes on a long journey for a religious purpose.

Jesus and the Pharisees

Matthew 23:13 *"How terrible for you, teachers of the law and Pharisees! You hypocrites! You lock the door to the kingdom of Heaven in people's faces."*

After clearing the money-changers and merchants out of the temple, Jesus spent the night in Bethany, a nearby village. The next day, he went back to the temple. This time, the Pharisees had set a trap for him. They sent some of their disciples to ask Jesus whether it was right for Jews to pay taxes to the Romans. They knew that if he said "yes", he would be very unpopular. If he said "no", he would be encouraging people to break the Roman law.

Jesus saw through them at once. He asked for a coin and then asked whose name and face were on it. "The Roman emperor's," he was told. "Then give then emperor what belongs to him," said Jesus, "and don't forget to give God what is due to him as well."

There were, as always, crowds of people in the temple, as well as the Pharisees and the teachers of the law. Speaking first to the people, Jesus told them that they should obey the law teachers and Pharisees, but that they should not follow their examples since these people did not do as they preached. They were hypocrites!

"Take a look at yourselves," Jesus told the law teachers and the Pharisees. "You have scripture verses on your clothing and you carry around books of God's word, yet you would not help your fellow man."

The religious leaders bowed their heads with embarrassment when Jesus continued. "These so-called men of God always take the best places at feasts and at the synagogue for themselves. They cannot properly encourage people to live good lives as they themselves do not live properly."

Jesus scolded the religious men for robbing the poor, acting unfairly and for following the laws of evil instead of the laws of the temple. He condemned them for making themselves seem good by giving God gifts and riches, while at the same time turning their backs on such important values as justice, honesty, and mercy.

As the scribes, law teachers, and Pharisees shuffled their feet and looked at the ground, Jesus turned to address the crowd, "These men might look like they are good people on the outside, but inside they are rotten!"

Finally, Jesus told the law teachers and Pharisees that they would be punished for their hypocrisy.

The Last Supper

At the end of the Passover celebrations, it was time for the Passover meal. Jesus knew that his enemies were looking for him, so the Passover meal to be shared with his friends would have to be held in secret. The disciples asked where Jesus wanted to have the meal, as Jerusalem was overcrowded. But many people were happy to share their homes with Jesus and he had already made arrangements for the meal that evening.

In reply to his disciples, Jesus said, "Go to the city and find a man carrying a jar of water. He will lead you to a house. Ask the owner of the house to show you the room upstairs where you can prepare the meal and we will eat there."

The disciples soon found the man carrying the water, as usually only women carried water.

Everything happened as Jesus had told them and they

prepared their meal in the upstairs room of the house.

That evening, Jesus and his disciples sat down to eat. In those days, the least important servant washed the feet of guests who had walked along dusty roads. A jug of water and towel lay ready, but no servants were present and not one of the disciples was prepared to do such a lowly job.

Jesus poured some water into a basin and picked up the towel. Then he knelt before each disciple and washed their feet.

When Jesus had finished his task, he said, "You see? I am prepared to do anything for you. You too must be ready to serve each other. Don't always think of yourselves and your own importance."

Later, as they sat at the table eating, drinking, and talking, Jesus looked around, and, smiling sadly, said, "One of you will betray me to my enemies."

The disciples were horrified. "You can't mean me?" asked each one.

When one of the disciples, Judas Iscariot, asked this, Jesus replied, "Yes, you are the one."

Then he broke a piece of bread and shared it with everyone. "This is my body," he said. "When you break and eat bread together like this, remember me."

Then Jesus passed a cup of wine among them. "Drink this, all of you," he said. "This is my blood, which will be poured out so that everyone's sins can be forgiven by God."

Did you know?

Today, people celebrate Passover by eating "matzo," a flat bread similar to the bread the Israelites ate after their departure from Egypt.

The Garden of Gethsemane

Luke 22:48 Jesus said, "Judas, is it with a kiss that you betray the Son of Man?"

Jesus and the disciples finished the Passover meal and then went for a walk to a quiet place outside the city.

"You will all run away from me," Jesus told them.

"Never!" exclaimed Peter. "I'd die with you if necessary."

The others all agreed.

Jesus shook his head. "Peter," he said, "before the cock crows tomorrow, three times you will have said that you don't know me."

"Never!" repeated Peter.

Jesus and his disciples reached a garden called Gethsemane.

Gathering his disciples, Jesus said, "Wait here while I pray. I am very sad. Please keep watch for me."

Walking a short distance away from the others, Jesus threw himself on the ground. "Please, Father!" he prayed, "don't let me suffer!"

Jesus prayed once more and spoke again, this time more calmly, "Don't do what I want, but do what You know is best."

Some time later, Jesus returned to his friends, who had fallen asleep. "Couldn't you have stayed awake for just one more hour?" he asked, disappointed. "Now you will have to wake up, because I'm going to be taken prisoner. Look! Here comes the one who has betrayed me."

A rough-looking crowd, including temple guards armed with sticks and spears, was walking toward them. At the front of the crowd was Judas Iscariot.

"The man I kiss is the one you want," he whispered to the guards, and walked boldly up to Jesus.

"Hello, Teacher," Judas said, and kissed Jesus on the cheek.

Jesus looked at Judas. "My friend," he said sadly, "are you betraying me with a kiss?"

Peter was furious as the guards rushed forward and seized Jesus. Pulling out a sword, Peter lashed out wildly, cutting a guard's ear.

"Put your sword away, Peter!" said Jesus. "If I wished to go free, I could call armies of angels to fight for me. But I am ready to give up my life according to God's plan."

Gently, Jesus reached out and touched the guard's bleeding ear, which healed instantly. Then he said to his captors, "Why are you treating me like a criminal? Every day I sat teaching in the temple, but you didn't arrest me then." The men did not answer.

Jesus knew that the priests who had him arrested were afraid of his crowd of followers. But as Jesus was taken out of the garden, his terrified disciples ran away.

Did you know?

The garden of Gethsemane is at the foot of the Mount of Olives in Jerusalem.

Peter Denies Jesus

Luke 22:56-57 She said: "This man was with him too," but he denied it, saying, "Woman, I do not know him."

The guards took Jesus to the house of Caiaphas, the high priest. It was still evening, but the priests had decided they must put Jesus on trial at once to avoid trouble from his followers.

Meanwhile, Peter and another disciple had stopped running. They suddenly realized how cowardly they were being and decided to follow the guards to see where Jesus was being taken.

When Peter and his companion reached the house of Caiaphas, they asked a servant girl at the gate if they could go in. "Yes," she answered, then looked closely at Peter. "Aren't you a disciple of that man?" she asked, pointing toward a room where Jesus had been taken.

"No, I am not!" replied Peter, afraid that he might be arrested for cutting the guard's ear. He shivered and made his way to warm his hands at the hot coal fire in the courtyard. A man standing nearby stared at Peter. "Aren't you one of that man's disciples?" he asked.

Afraid of what might happen to him if the conversation was overheard, Peter bowed his head and replied, "No, I am not!"

In the corner of the courtyard, some servants were discussing the latest events. They looked across at Peter and one called out, "You are one of the prisoner's friends. You can't deny it, I saw you with him—and you come from Galilee, too. You have the same accent!"

Everyone stared at Peter, who lost his temper. "I tell you, I don't know who you're talking about," he shouted angrily.

Just then, dawn began to light up the dark sky and somewhere a cock crowed. Peter remembered what Jesus had said to him a few hours earlier: "Before the cock crows tomorrow, three times you will have said that you don't know me."

Ashamed, Peter looked through the window to where Jesus was standing, being questioned by his enemies. Jesus looked back at him kindly. Peter felt terrible. He had failed someone who had never let him down. He rushed out of the courtyard, crying bitterly.

Did you know?

Peter is one of the most important of Jesus' twelve disciples, and Jesus calls him his "rock." He was the first to call Jesus "the Messiah," which means "anointed by God."

The Trial of Jesus

> Mark 15:9-10 *"Do you want me to set free for you the king of the Jews?" He knew very well that the chief priests had handed Jesus over to him because they were jealous.*

Jesus was blindfolded and beaten and put on trial before the Council of Jewish leaders. The council tried hard to prove his guilt, but none of the witnesses told the same story. Then the high priest, Caiaphas, demanded of Jesus, "Are you the Son of God?"

"I am," replied Jesus.

"Ha!" answered Caiaphas. "We don't need any more witnesses. He has said he is like a god, and for this he deserves to die."

Only the Romans were allowed to put people to death, so Jesus was sent to the Roman governor, Pontius Pilate. "This troublemaker tells people not to pay taxes and says he is their king," the priests told him.

If this was true, Jesus could be sentenced to death, but Pilate was sure the religious leaders had made up the charges because they were jealous of Jesus.

"Are you the king of the Jews?" Pilate asked. But Jesus would answer no more questions.

Pilate was sure Jesus was innocent, but outside his palace the priests were stirring up trouble and people were chanting, "Crucify him!" Pilate had an idea.

"It's Passover," he called to the mob. "As part of the celebrations, I always set one prisoner free. This man has done nothing to deserve death, so shall he be set free?"

"No!" yelled the crowd. "Free Barabbas, instead!" Barabbas was in prison for murder. Pilate shrugged and ordered his soldiers to set Barabbas free.

Meanwhile, other soldiers beat Jesus and forced a crown of thorny twigs onto his head. They wrapped a purple cloak around him, and jeered, "Long live the King!"

At last, Pilate took Jesus out to the crowd. The same people who had welcomed Jesus into Jerusalem only five days before now roared, "Let him die on the cross!"

Did you know?

Crucifixion was a painful public punishment, meant to warn onlookers not to commit similar crimes.

The Crucifixion

Jesus was led away to die. Under Jewish law, he had to be killed outside the city gates. The Roman soldiers made him carry the heavy wooden cross to a place called Golgotha. A mocking crowd followed and Jesus, weak from being questioned and beaten, stumbled beneath the weight of the cross.

A broad-shouldered man was there called Simon, who had come from North Africa for Passover,

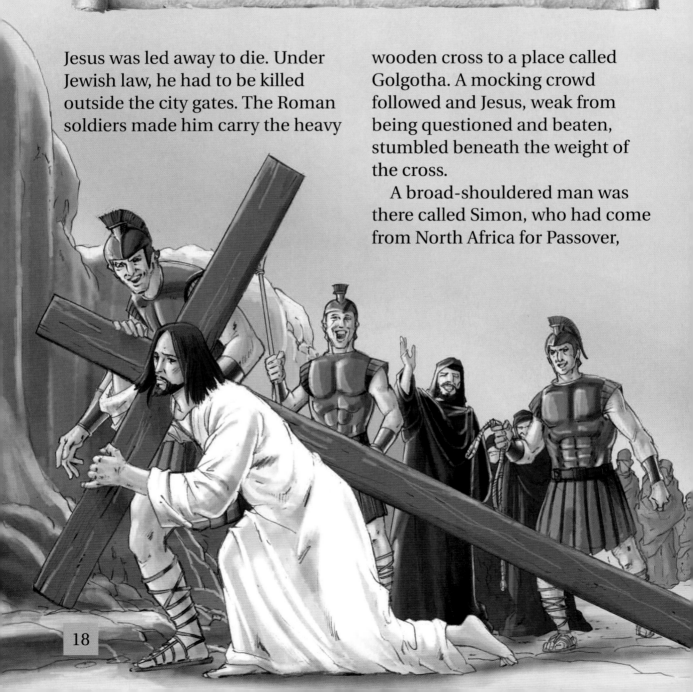

18

and the soldiers grabbed him. "Carry the cross for the prisoner," they called, "or we'll never get there." Simon helped Jesus for the rest of the way to Golgotha. Then the words "The King of the Jews" were written on the cross.

When they reached the hill, the soldiers laid Jesus down on the cross and hammered nails through his feet and wrists. Jesus said, "Father, forgive them, for they do not realize what they are doing."

Two robbers were put on crosses on either side of him. The crosses were set into the ground and lifted up, so that the men would die from heat and thirst. It was nine o'clock in the morning, so the soldiers sat down and began gambling with dice to pass the time until the prisoners died.

When the religious leaders arrived, they taunted, "You saved others, but you can't save yourself."

Then one of the two robbers called out, "Aren't you the Chosen One? Save yourself and us!"

"Don't say that," interrupted the other robber. "We are both getting what we deserve, but this man has done nothing wrong!" Then turning toward Jesus, he said, "Remember me when you reach your kingdom."

"Today you will be with me in Paradise," replied Jesus.

Some of Jesus' friends were there, crying. Jesus whispered down to John, "Look after my mother and be a son to her."

At midday, when the sun should have been at its brightest, the sky turned black and Jesus called out, "My God, why have you deserted me?" By three o'clock, he gasped, "I'm so thirsty!"

A soldier soaked a sponge in sour wine and held it up to moisten Jesus' dry lips. Then in a clear voice, Jesus said, "It's finished!"

At that moment, back in Jerusalem, the curtain in the temple was torn in two. At Golgotha, Jesus bowed his head and died.

Did you know?

The name Christ comes from the Greek word "Christos." Like "Messiah," it means "anointed" or "chosen one."

Jesus Rises from the Grave

Pontius Pilate agreed that two of Jesus' followers could give him a proper burial. They took his body, wrapped it in strips of cloth, and took it to a garden where a new grave had been cut into a rock. The Pharisees were worried that the disciples would steal the body and pretend that Jesus had risen, so they sealed the tomb and Roman soldiers stood guard over it.

Some of the women who had been Jesus' friends watched the burial. Worn out with sadness and crying, they left. It was Friday evening and the next day was the Sabbath, the Jewish day of rest. They could do nothing but mourn and wait for the day to pass.

As soon as Saturday evening came, the women began preparing perfumes and spices to put on Jesus' body. They wanted to show how much they cared for him.

Early on Sunday morning, Mary Magdalene and some of the other women made their way to the garden. When they arrived, the guards had gone and the huge rock sealing the grave had been moved aside, leaving the tomb wide open.

Mary Magdalene ran to get Peter and John. They peered inside the cave. On the floor lay the grave clothes but Jesus' body had gone. Peter and John went back to the other disciples but Mary remained, tears pouring down her cheeks. She looked into the tomb again and saw two angels, sitting where Jesus' body had been.

"Why are you crying?" asked a man's voice. She had not noticed anyone else in the garden and supposed he was the gardener. "Sir," she replied, "they have moved Jesus' body. Do you know where it is?"

"Mary!" exclaimed the man, and suddenly she recognized him. It was Jesus.

"Master!" she cried.

"Go and tell my disciples that I have risen and am on my way to our Father," said Jesus, smiling.

Mary ran out of the garden, her sadness lifted. She burst in on the grieving group of disciples and cried, "He's alive! He's really alive!"

> ## Did you know?
>
> The Jewish Sabbath is from sunset on Friday to sunset on Saturday. It recalls the creation of the world by God in six days, while on the seventh He rested.

Jesus Visits his Disciples

Luke 24:30-31 As he sat down to eat with them, he took some bread, blessed it, then broke it and gave it to them. And their eyes were opened, and they knew him; and he vanished out of their sight.

On the afternoon when Jesus rose again, two of his disciples were walking home to the nearby village of Emmaus when a stranger caught up with them. "You look sad," he said. "What's wrong?"

"Haven't you heard about Jesus of Nazareth?" said one of the disciples. "We thought that he had been sent by God, but he's been put to death."

"Some women said that they had seen him, alive, but he was dead when they took him down from the cross," said the second disciple.

"Now his body has disappeared from his tomb," added the first.

The stranger replied, "But our holy writings say that God's promised king must die and rise again."

The stranger continued talking about the meanings of the scriptures and, in no time, they had reached the disciples' home.

"Come in, stranger!" urged the disciples. "Have supper with us."

At the table, the stranger thanked God and passed round the bread. Suddenly, the disciples recognized the stranger. It was Jesus!

The two men rushed back to Jerusalem to tell the other disciples. Before they could speak, the disciples cried "Jesus has risen! Peter has seen him!" Then the two men told the other disciples they had met Jesus too.

Suddenly, Jesus was in the room. He explained that soon the disciples would have to tell everyone that he had died and come alive again so that the sins of mankind could be forgiven.

22

The Miraculous Catch of Fish

John 21:6 And he said to them, "Cast your net on the right side of the boat, and see what you find." When they did so, they were not able to pull the net up, there were so many fish in it.

One evening in Galilee, Peter went fishing with James, John, Thomas, and some of the other disciples.

But as night passed and daybreak came, they hadn't caught a single fish. On the shore, a man cupped his hands and called across the lake to them, "Cast your net to the right!"

Something about him made the disciples obey. They tossed their net to the right and at once it was weighed down with fish.

"That's Jesus!" John said to Peter. Peter leapt into the water and swam! By the time he reached the shore, Jesus was already cooking some fish.

"Bring more fish!" said Jesus, so Peter went to meet the boat and helped to haul the heavy net ashore.

When the friends counted the fish, there were one hundred and fifty-three! The disciples tucked into the bread and grilled fish that Jesus had prepared, then Peter walked along the shore with Jesus.

Three times, Jesus asked Peter the same question, "Peter, do you love me?"

Peter felt ashamed, remembering how he had lied three times about knowing Jesus. "Yes," answered Peter, sadly.

"Then look after my followers," said Jesus.

Peter realized that Jesus had forgiven him as he had given him an important job to do.

23

The Ascension

For forty days, Jesus appeared to his friends at different times. He looked and seemed different, but there was no doubt that he was alive. He ate meals with the disciples and talked with them as he had done before he was crucified. But now he could pass through closed doors and appear or disappear at will. He helped the disciples to understand a lot more about the scriptures than they had before.

On the fortieth day after he had risen in the garden, he walked with them to the Mount of Olives and turned to them. "You must tell everyone all about what has happened," he said. "Go and preach the Gospel everywhere, and make your own disciples, baptizing them in the name of the Father, the Son, and the Holy Spirit. Once people understand why I suffered and died, then rose again, they will live better lives."

Jesus held up his hands to bless them and spoke once more. "Remember that I will be with you always, just as I always told you." Then he rose up into the sky and disappeared behind a cloud. The disciples returned to Jerusalem and went to the temple every day to thank God for Jesus.

One morning, six weeks later, Jerusalem was once more packed with pilgrims, as they had all come to celebrate the festival of Pentecost, the harvest thanksgiving for the first ripe crops.

Something strange happened. The disciples were in a house, when a rushing wind suddenly blew through the rooms. Then, just for an instant, a small tongue of flame settled on every disciple. Warmth surged through them and they realized that this was the Holy Spirit, sent from Heaven.

A large crowd had gathered outside the house. The people had seen and heard the wind and wondered what was happening. The disciples stepped outside, feeling happy for the first time in weeks. But what happened then was even more amazing. Everyone in the street, no matter what country they had come from, understood perfectly what the disciples were saying.

Did you know?

The Feast of the Ascension is the day that Christians commemorate the rising of Jesus to Heaven. It is usually celebrated on the fortieth day after Easter Sunday.

The Early Church

Peter and the other disciples taught more people about Jesus, baptizing them as Jesus had done. Thousands of people became new disciples and met in each other's houses to pray together. Their happiness spread, and even more people began joining them.

One afternoon, Peter and John were going to the Temple when they met a lame beggar. He sat beside the temple gates each day, calling, "Give me some money! I can't walk. Give me some money so that I can buy food!"

Peter and John stopped. They saw this man every day, but had not yet spoken to him.

"I haven't any money to give you," said Peter, "but I'll give you what I have. In the name of Jesus Christ, get up and walk!"

Peter helped the beggar to stand and at once the beggar felt strength flow into his feet and ankles. He let go of Peter's hand and started to walk. Then he began to run and jump, shouting, "Look, I can walk! How good God is. Thank you, God!"

The beggar ran into the temple where everyone who knew him was amazed to see him walking about and praising God.

The First Martyr

*Acts 7:60 Then he fell on his knees and cried aloud,
"Lord, do not hold this sin against them." And with that he died.*

The disciples gave help to those who needed it, but so much time was taken up with caring for the needy that they did not have enough time to preach and pray as Jesus had asked them to do.

Eventually, the disciples picked seven men to take charge of sharing out the funds they raised among those in need.

Among the men chosen was Stephen, who argued with the Pharisees very skilfully to prove that Jesus was the Messiah. This infuriated them. "He must be stopped!" they said. "He is going against the way we've followed God for centuries."

The Pharisees made up false charges against him and put him on trial.

Bravely, Stephen stood before the Pharisees and said, "You rejected and murdered Jesus, God's own son." This made the Pharisees angry and they threatened to kill Stephen, too.

Stephen simply said, "I can see Jesus in Heaven, standing at God's side." At this, the leaders, including a young Pharisee called Saul, dragged him out of the city. They picked up stones and hurled them at Stephen. Falling to his knees, he prayed, "Lord Jesus, take me to you!"

Just before he died, Stephen said, "Forgive them for this crime."

Saul is Converted

Acts 9:5 "Saul, Saul, why do you persecute me?" "Tell me, Lord," he said, "who you are." The voice answered, "I am Jesus."

Saul was proud to be a Pharisee and was determined to stop people following Jesus. One day, he set off for Damascus to try and capture some of Jesus' supporters and bring them back to Jerusalem. On the way, a dazzling light shone all around him and made him blind.

From nowhere, he heard a voice, "Saul, why are you attacking me?"

Terrified, Saul asked, "Who are you?"

"I am Jesus," came the reply. "When you attack my followers, you attack me."

"What do you want me to do, Lord?" Saul asked, his hatred gone.

"Go to Damascus and you will be told," said Jesus.

The men who were accompanying Saul to Damascus were puzzled and wondered who Saul was talking to; they could hear a voice but could not see anyone

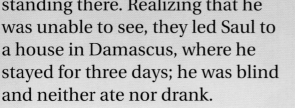

standing there. Realizing that he was unable to see, they led Saul to a house in Damascus, where he stayed for three days; he was blind and neither ate nor drank.

Jesus appeared in a vision to one of his followers, a man named Ananias, and told him to go to see Saul. Ananias was horrified at this. "But Saul is our enemy," he said.

Jesus explained that he had chosen Saul to become his follower, so Ananias went to the house where Saul was staying and spoke kindly to him. At once, Saul felt a strange sensation, as though something like fish scales were falling from his eyes—and suddenly he could see again! Then Ananias baptized him as a sign that he now followed Jesus.

Saul began to tell everyone he could about God and Jesus, but this made Saul's own people become his bitter enemies. They watched the city gates, planning to capture him and kill him. But one night, Saul's new friends lowered him over the city walls in a basket and he escaped.

Did you know?

Saul was a clever man who spoke Greek and Latin. He was also known by the Latin and Greek name "Paul."

ARCTURUS

This edition published in 2012 by Arcturus Publishing Limited
26/27 Bickels Yard, 151–153 Bermondsey Street, London SE1 3HA

Designed by Moseley Strachan

ISBN: 978-1-84858-016-9

CH002591US

Supplier 15, Date 1012, Print run 2271

Printed in China